THERE IS A
REWARD
—— FOR ——
PARENTING

THERE IS A
REWARD
—— FOR ——
PARENTING

© Oluwakemi. O. Ola - Ojo 2010

There Is A Reward For Parenting.

ISBN 978-0-9557898-6-1
Copyright© 2010 by OLUWAKEMI. O. OLA-OJO

All publishing rights belong exclusively to Protokos Publishers.

Published by
Protokos Publishers
P.O. Box 48424
London
SE15 2YL
Website: www.protokospublishers.com

Printed in the United Kingdom. All rights reserved under International Copyright Law. Contents and or cover may not be reproduced in whole or in part in any form without the express written consent of the Publisher.

Unless otherwise stated, all scripture quotations in this book are from the King James Version of the Bible.

Cover design by **Prex Nigeria Limited**
e-mail: prexng_2000@yahoo.com

CONTENTS

DEDICATION

ACKNOWLEDGEMENT

FOREWORD

INTRODUCTION

CHAPTER 1   **EVERY CHILD COUNTS**

CHAPTER 2   **THE MAKING OF A WINNER**

CHAPTER 3   **YOU NEED WISDOM**

CHAPTER 4   **GOOD AND BAD PARENTING**

POEMS

    GOD'S GIFT YOU CAN NEVER BUY

    TOUCH SOMEONE TODAY

    DESPISE THEM NOT

    NOBODY EVER KNOWS

    WHY THE STIGMA?

    I LOVED THEM BOTH DEARLY

    TRAIN THEM OR LOSE THEM

    WHERE ARE THE GOOD FATHER'S TODAY?

DEDICATION

To:
all the parents who take time to bring up their children in the fear of the Lord,
&
all the teachers who invest in children, the word and love of God.

ACKNOWLEDGEMENT

With all of my heart, soul and being, I acknowledge Jesus Christ who knocked on the door of my heart as an 8 year old and came into my life during a Sunday evening service. He introduced me to God the Father and to the Holy Spirit, now my best friend, mentor, teacher, instructor, and guide.

I am grateful to my Godly parents for taking me to Church from birth and for loving the Lord in their everyday life.

My appreciation goes to Children Evangelism Ministry, The Shepherd's Ministries and Teenagers' Outreach Ministries for teaching me how to minister to, and reach out to children and young adults. My thanks also extend to Rev. Yemi Ladokun for spotting my writing skills early. It was a privilege to serve under her Godly leadership in the Lydia Auxiliary of Nigerian Baptist Convention.

For giving me the opportunity to serve and share God's word and His love with children, I say thanks to the entire

Children's Sunday School Coordinators. To the children whose lives has been positively enhanced by God's word and love. I count myself priviledged and I say thank you.

To Mrs Bisi Chukwudile, I cannot but thank her for her help and for finding time to write the foreword in spite of her very busy schedule.

To the management and staff of Prex Holdings for the excellent editing and book covers and to Protokos Publishers for helping to get this into print and marketing my books, I say 'Thank you all.'

Finally, but not in the least, my thanks go to Pastor Tony Taiwo, whose request brought about the admonition in this book.

FOREWORD

Oluwakemi Ojo has written, not just a book, but with her very expressive and passionate poems, she has written many books in one. I admonish every parent to take time to carefully read this excellent book.

As someone who has been in children's work for some decades, I was pleasantly delighted to find out that there were many nuggets for me to glean from her book. I recommend this book not only to parents and children workers but to the people in government, medical and school work, indeed to anyone who is a stake holder in the welfare of Today's Child.

Bisi Chukwudile
International Mission Director
Children Evangelism Ministry Headquarters.

INTRODUCTION

In May 1999, Pastor Tony Taiwo asked that I bring a word of admonition to parents during the Children's week of Christ Faith Tabernacle, London. This book has been written from that sharing. The message is still as relevant today as it was then. God's charge to us either as parents or teachers is to nurse each child for Him and He will surely reward each one of us.

Children are so important to God that He has a place for them in His heart and agenda. Whilst the disciples, like many churches today, drove the children away thinking the Messiah only came for adults, Jesus rebuked them and called the children to Him, holding, hugging and blessing them (Mark 13:13-16). When the question arose as to who was the greatest in the kingdom of heaven, Jesus chose a child to get His reply across to the disciples:

> *At the same time came the disciples unto Jesus, saying, Who is the greatest in the kingdom of heaven? And Jesus called a little child unto him,*

and set him in the midst of them, And said, Verily I say unto you, Except ye be converted, and become as little children, ye shall not enter into the kingdom of heaven. Whosoever therefore shall humble himself as this little child, the same is greatest in the kingdom of heaven.

And whoso shall receive one such little child in my name receiveth me. But whoso shall offend one of these little ones which believe in me, it were better for him that a millstone were hanged about his neck, and that he were drowned in the depth of the sea. Take heed that ye despise not one of these little ones; for I say unto you, That in heaven their angels do always behold the face of my Father which is in heaven. –

Matthew 18: 1-6, 10

Jesus stressed the need for the disciples to receive children in His name and more importantly He warned them not to lead any child astray. As a parent, teacher, church or community leader, how are you treating the children in your care? Are many churches today not as guilty as the disciples were in the accommodation assigned to the Children and Youth arms of their ministries; in the quality of teachers assigned to them during service times, and in the facilities and tools made available for the children and youth departments?

Some churches have budgets for every department but not the Children and Youth departments. They expect the teachers and perhaps a handful of generous parents to foot the bill to meet the needs of those arms of the church.

The Church is meant to be a haven for everyone who comes in. However many who have come (children inclusive) to seek for refuge, protection, love and care have been abused by some Church people including those who wear priestly garments and robes.

While most parents will not send their children to poorly staffed secular schools, they leave the spiritual training of their children to Sunday school teachers who are ill equipped to teach, train or minister to the spiritual, yea, other needs of their children. No wonder many of the children who pass through such Sunday schools rebel against the church and God at the slightest opportunity. In the home, the child is to be taught the love and sovereignty of God, good family values which are fundamental to the society. In the Church, the child needs to learn and be motivated to live a God fearing, fruitful, fulfilling and purposeful life.

In the school, the child should be taught the truth about

each subject. A society that has its foundation based on lies such as the big bang theory cannot escape corruption, wickedness and all the vile we see today. The child needs to know truths including the fact that God created the world, has and will continue to sustain it, the flood did happen in Noah's time etc. Good children are not only the hope and future of any society; they are God's great gift as well.

Any organisation or church is only as strong as its foundation. This book has been written amongst other things to raise all parents and the church out of their slumber, make them reorder their priorities and pay more attention to the children God has entrusted in their care.

Perhaps you are wondering what qualifies me for writing such a book – God by His anointing, Holy Spirit by inspiration, Word of God by examples, the experiences of my grandmother, mother and myself in raising children, my experience at work, from my friends and social network and experience as a Sunday school teacher and youth worker for over two decades.

At the end of the book, I have included some inspiring poems, which the Lord gave to me at different times in the past concerning the unique place of children in His divine agenda, and other related issues. Do read and be specially blessed.

EVERY CHILD COUNTS

No child chooses to be born at all let alone decide which family he or she is born into and when. The best of family planning methods cannot stop God from giving couples children when He decides to do so. Man may claim that the conception of a particular child was accidental, but in God's eyes every child is in His plan and has a purpose and mission to fulfil on the earth.

The truth of the above claim is aptly illustrated in the account of the circumstances surrounding Moses' birth and early childhood. His story will be the reference point for all that will be discussed here and in subsequent chapters of this book.

Text:
> *Now these are the names of the children of Israel, which came into Egypt; every man and his household came with Jacob. Reuben, Simeon, Levi, and Judah, Issachar, Zebulun, and Benjamin, Dan, and Naphtali, Gad, and Asher. And all the*

souls that came out of the loins of Jacob were seventy souls: for Joseph was in Egypt already.

And Joseph died, and all his brethren, and all that generation. And the children of Israel were fruitful, and increased abundantly, and multiplied, and waxed exceedingly mighty; and the land was filled with them. Now there arose up a new king over Egypt, which knew not Joseph. And he said unto his people, Behold, the people of the children of Israel are more and mightier than we:

Come on, let us deal wisely with them; lest they multiply, and it come to pass, that, when there falleth out any war, they join also unto our enemies, and fight against us, and so get them up out of the land. Therefore they did set over them taskmasters to afflict them with their burdens. And they built for Pharaoh treasure cities, Pithom and Raamses. But the more they afflicted them, the more they multiplied and grew. And they were grieved because of the children of Israel.

And the Egyptians made the children of Israel to serve with rigour: And they made their lives bitter with hard bondage, in mortar, and in brick, and in all manner of service in the field: all their service, wherein they made them serve, was with rigour. And the king of Egypt spake to the Hebrew midwives, of which the name of the one was Shiphrah, and the name of the other Puah:

And he said, When ye do the office of a midwife to the Hebrew women, and see them upon the stools; if it be a son, then ye shall kill him: but if it be a daughter, then she shall live.

But the midwives feared God, and did not as the king of Egypt commanded them, but saved the men children alive. And the king of Egypt called for the midwives, and said unto them, Why have ye done this thing, and have saved the men children alive? And the midwives said unto Pharaoh, Because the Hebrew women are not as the Egyptian women; for they are lively, and are delivered ere the midwives come in unto them. Therefore God dealt well with the midwives: and the people multiplied, and waxed very mighty.

And it came to pass, because the midwives feared God, that he made them houses. And Pharaoh charged all his people, saying, Every son that is born ye shall cast into the river, and every daughter ye shall save alive.

And there went a man of the house of Levi, and took to wife a daughter of Levi. And the woman conceived, and bare a son: and when she saw him that he was a goodly child, she hid him three months. And when she could not longer hide him, she took for him an ark of bulrushes, and daubed it with slime and with pitch, and put the child therein; and she laid it in the flags by the river's brink.

And his sister stood afar off, to wit what would be done to him. And the daughter of Pharaoh came down to wash herself at the river; and her maidens walked along by the river's side; and when she saw the ark among the flags, she sent her maid to fetch it. And when she had opened it, she saw the child: and, behold, the babe wept. And she had compassion on him, and said, This is one of the Hebrews' children. Then said his sister to Pharaoh's daughter, Shall I go and call to thee a nurse of the Hebrew women, that she may nurse the child for thee? And Pharaoh's daughter said to her, Go. And the maid went and called the child's mother.

And Pharaoh's daughter said unto her, Take this child away, and nurse it for me, and I will give thee thy wages. And the woman took the child, and nursed it. And the child grew, and she brought him unto Pharaoh's daughter, and he became her son. And she called his name Moses: and she said, Because I drew him out of the water. (Exodus 1: 1 – end; Exodus 2: 1- 10)

GLADLY ACCEPT THAT CHILD

What should have been a happy celebration turned out for Amran and his wife, Jochebed, a trying and difficult time *(Exodus 2:2).* It must have been particularly difficult for Jochebed who like any mother had no say in the sex of the child that God gave her. Even the best of medicine today cannot guarantee 100% a particular sex. The timing of Moses' birth was not ideal but nowhere in the Bible is it recorded that his mother complained, or murmured to God for giving her a male child who by the decree at the time was destined for death. Jochebed gladly accepted her child.

Over the years in my professional experience, I have observed that many of the problematic pregnancies are strategic children of either sex. For these children, the battle for survival starts from the womb and it takes God and using the available good medical care for them to be born alive and healthy. I don't know why and perhaps this is worth researching. The fight in Revelations chapter 12 between the dragon and the woman was over the life of her son. If not for God's help she would have lost the baby. That was a strategic child, which even before birth was a threat to Satan hence the vehement attacks.

God matches everything about a person to their destiny including their sex. It would have been most unlikely for Moses at that time to lead the children of God out of Egypt if he was a woman. How sad it is to see some parents unhappy about the sex of their child. It is an act of wickedness and ingratitude to God who has given them a healthy child. A million and one things could have gone wrong with that pregnancy resulting in a maimed or dead child or mother or both! Such parents act as if they are smarter than God and know the future of their child. They are ignorant of the faithfulness of God. If you are one of such parents, repent now and ask God for His forgiveness and mercy. Ask for His grace to love your child from now on.

Also, couples ought to be careful not to allow prevailing circumstances to make them label a pregnancy 'not convenient', 'unwanted' or a 'mistake'. These are statements that they may regret in future. There is no mistake with God, which is why every conception happened in the first instance. He knows every child before he or she is formed in the womb. *(Jeremiah 1:4-5; Psalm 139:13-16)*

God did not reveal to Amran and his wife the destiny of their child just as He also may choose not reveal to you the destiny of your child today. But Jochebed saw that her child was a fine boy. Another translation says 'beautiful child' *(Exodus 2:2)*. This was her third child and second son yet she found time to appreciate the baby's unique beauty. Parents, please take time to appreciate each of your children:

Lo, children are an heritage of the Lord: and the fruit of the womb is his reward. As arrows are in the hand of a mighty man; so are children of the youth. Happy is the man that hath his quiver full of them: they shall not be ashamed, but they shall speak with the enemies in the gate.
- Psalm 127:3-5

Each child is a unique gift from God and there should be no comparison with any other person within or outside the family, dead or alive. After all, even identical twins don't have the same destiny despite the fact that they are genetically alike and come from the same egg.

THE MALE SEED

For over 300 years the children of Israel resided peacefully in Egypt until the reign of a new Pharaoh who was afraid of the increasing number and exceeding strength of the

Israelites. To limit their number and break their spirit, Pharaoh appointed taskmasters to oppress them with increasingly hard labour. When this did not work, he decreed that all the newborn baby boys were to be thrown into the Nile *(Exodus 1:22).*

The male seed is so important in the continuity of life and the defence of it, which is why boys often times are the targets of the enemy in any family, culture, or society that he wants to terminate. For instance, the majority of the people who go to war are male. Also, the higher number of men compared to women inmates in prisons confirms that males are more prone to negative ends.

Eliminating the boys by Pharaoh's decree would make Israel no more a threat to the Egyptians. It was during this frightening period that Moses was born. His parents were from the tribe of Levi – the tribe chosen by God to be His Priests but despite their high calling and anointing, they were not immune from Pharaoh's ungodly decree. In the same way today, children of Christian parents are sometimes victims of enemy attacks. The devil has not changed his strategy; he has only repackaged the method.

LET GO AND LET GOD

In love for her son, Moses' biological mother hid him for three months, nursing him secretly rather than giving him up to be thrown into the Nile. Then came a time when she could no longer hide him and had to give him up. In the same way, there comes a time, when every mother will have to let go of her child to let God take over. It might be frightening and worrisome but until you let go, God may not step in.

Putting her trust in God, Jochebed prayerfully planned how to give up her son. Instead of just throwing him into the Nile as decreed, she made a waterproof papyrus basket, plastered with bitumen and pitch: it was eye-catching and comfortable like a little ship. She put her baby in it and placed it among the reeds in a fairly secure part of the River Nile, while her daughter stood at a distance to see what would happen to the basket *(Exodus 2:3-4).*

To show that no sex is superior to the other, Miriam, a girl, was very instrumental in the preservation of the life of Moses. Every boy or girl has a place in the world in the plan of God, a destiny to fulfil, a work to do that no one else but him or her can do.

By God's divine appointment and intervention, Pharaoh's daughter came to bathe in the same river, saw the baby boy crying in the basket and took pity on him *(Exodus 2:5-6)*. God's perfect timing made all these possible. God hears the cries of children too and so parents ought to teach their children how to cry to God and praise Him as early as possible in life *(Genesis 21:15-17)*. God never leaves His own, no wonder the Psalmist said, even though he walks through the darkest valley he fears no evil for God is with him and His rod and staff both comfort him *(Psalm 23:4)*.

The same water that killed other boys spared Moses' life. The same king that ordered all boys of his age to be killed adopted Moses to be brought up within the walls of the palace. When the Lord steps into a situation, what was meant to kill and destroy becomes the stepping-stone to victory, protection, provision and fame.

By divine arrangement, Pharaoh's daughter decided to appoint a Hebrew woman as the boy's nurse. His sister Miriam went and called their mother to do the job and she, within the little time she had to care for her son, laid the foundation for him to be a winner and leader. She must have told him about Jehovah, the only true God. She possibly told him about the plight of the Hebrews and their desire for a leader who will be used of Jehovah to deliver them from oppression and bondage. Pharaoh's daughter would definitely not have told Moses all these things.

Up until Moses' ride in the basket on the river, he was like any other Hebrew male child, destined to die according to the prevailing law at that time. He was not from an extraordinary or wealthy family but one divine encounter with the Princess of the land changed his story. His life was spared: he was immediately adopted by the Princess therefore gaining access to the best nurse – his mother; and to the throne of Egypt and all that it stood for – the world power of their day.

The wealth and security of Pharaoh was used in nursing and bringing up Israel's deliverer! What a mighty God we serve indeed.

THE MAKING OF A WINNER

Take this child away, and nurse it for me, and I will give thee thy wages…

- Exodus 2:9

As Pharaoh's daughter said to Moses' mother, so God says to every parent today, take this child away, and nurse [him/her] for me, and I will give thee thy wages.

TAKE THAT CHILD

To take in this context means to accept, accommodate, carry, and understand the child just as he or she is without complaint. Not every child will be exceptionally brilliant, athletic or artistic. Nevertheless look for the God-given qualities in each of your children and commend such. Love the child and avoid destructive comparison. What you think is a weakness, when given to God, will become strength. Moses did not have any male peers as they had all been killed by the ungodly decree. There was a difference of four and eight years respectively between Moses and his brother Aaron and sister Miriam. From personal experience, not having other children of the same age around a toddler can sometimes affect how soon that child will be able to crawl, walk and talk. For whatever reasons, Moses grew up as a stammerer.

It is a known fact that children who stammer often end up being quiet, reserved, nervous in public and shy. A good example is Benny Hinn, one of the leading men of God today who shares his experience as a stammerer in his book, Good Morning Holy Spirit. How easy it would have been for Moses' mother to compare him with eloquent Aaron his elder brother but she did not *(Exodus 4:10 -16)*. No one can understand God; His ways are mysterious. In the same family, one was an eloquent speaker, while the other stammered.

Please avoid comments such as, "If only you could be like your brother in this or like your sister in that." Such statements, rather than build up, destroy, for the child may think that he or she is no good, or will only be wanted and loved on performance basis. God loves each of us just as we are and so should we love our children.

FOCUS ON STRENGTHS

Whatever physical, medical or educational defect a child has does not remove the fact that God lovingly made him or her and has a plan for his or her life. It is your responsibility as a parent to look for the strengths of your child and leave God to sort out the weaknesses or deficiencies. God never makes a mistake in His creation. Each human being is unique: wonderfully and fearfully made (Psalm 139: 13-18). What more, we are all under God's construction whilst still on planet earth.

Some children who are not athletic, when loved unconditionally and taught about God can be involved in creative thinking and writing that will make them achieve greater fame than their sporty counterparts. Similarly, children who are not particularly brilliant at school may find fulfilment leaving their indelible mark in athletics or business. Ask God to help you as a parent or teacher to learn how to unconditionally accept every child. From my little experience of life, the despised child with the help of God and many times with his or her determination often ends up being the one who sustains the family at critical times.

Moses' elder siblings, his entire family and the nation of Israel found their destiny fulfilled in Moses, the one the devil wanted to eliminate. The eloquent and older ones now had to serve under their younger and stammering brother *(Exodus 4:10-6).* Never underestimate your child; he could be another Joseph – the deliverer in famine, *(Genesis 45);* or David the youngest in the family but the only man after God's own heart and anointed king, *(1 Samuel 16);* or Solomon the product of an adulterous relationship yet the wisest and richest King *(2 Samuel 12:1-24; 1 Kings 1 – 4);* or Jephthah the unloved and unwanted brother who turned out to be a mighty warrior and deliverer *(Judges 11).*

NURSE YOUR CHILD

To nurse in this context means to breast-feed, care for, cherish, encourage, nourish, nurture, promote, support, sustain, and tend a child physically, emotionally, socially and spiritually. It is understandable where for medical reasons a mother is not allowed to breast feed her child, unfortunately, some parents abandon their responsibility right from the stage of breast-feeding.

Some mothers deny their baby of divinely provided breast milk for very flimsy reasons such as wanting to maintain the shape of their breasts! They refuse to consider the effect of this denial on the life and future of the child. For instance, research shows that breast-feeding strengthens a baby's immune system, facilitates brain development, helps to prevent obesity and reduces the risk of ear infection and sudden infant death syndrome. It might even reduce the baby's risk of developing heart disease in adulthood.

Providing breast milk is one basic part of nursing a child but there is more to it than that.

ROOTS ARE IMPORTANT

The Bible does not tell us how many years Moses spent with his mother but it certainly was limited. By the time Pharaoh's daughter gave Moses to his biological mother to nurse she had adopted him and so in principle he was an Egyptian. But whatever the length of time that Moses had with his biological mother, it was enough for her to impart to him, among other things, his roots as a Hebrew child *(Exodus 2:11-13).*

It is disheartening when non-citizens residing in foreign lands refuse to teach their children about their indigenous culture and mother tongue. That a child is born and raised in another country, possibly a richer one compared to your place of origin and having that country's birth certificate does not and cannot change the child's original root. The home is a child's first school. A building is only as strong as the foundation. What we teach our children in the first few years of their lives at home matters a lot.

Parents, please spend meaningful, purposeful time with your children. Take time to teach them about their roots especially the good things about their rich culture. Teach them to eat your food, wear your traditional clothes (weather permitting), understand, speak and be able to read and write your language. No culture is more superior to the other. God did not make a mistake about your origin. Appreciate it and celebrate it so long as it does not contradict the word of the Lord. The 'Moses' in your child needs to know and identify with his or her roots otherwise God's calling may never be realised in his or her life.

TEACH THE WORD

As parents, the time we have with our children is limited for soon it will be necessary for them to go to school, college or university, get married and so on. We ought to make the best use of the time that we have now (Proverbs 22:6). Children can and are able to understand the message of the gospel if we but teach them. They don't lack intelligence they simply lack teachers. Remember the admonition in Deuteronomy 6:7 and be careful to obey it:

And thou shalt teach them diligently unto thy children, and shalt talk of them when thou sittest in thine house, and when thou liest down, and when thou risest up.

The greatest investment parents can make in their children is to teach and train them in the way of the Lord particularly before the world starts bombarding them with ungodly information. Don't be afraid to take your children to Church, Sunday school and fellowship meetings. They are not too young to know and understand their maker.

Don't just take your child to Church or house fellowship, be sure they are sitting in and participating in the service. The decline in the moral standards that is prevalent in society today is proportional to the decline of the truth as contained in the Bible that today's youth know, believe and practise.

TEACH HONOURING GOD

The Bible has many examples of children and young adults who feared the Lord and honoured Him even in circumstances where they could have easily disobeyed His commandments. For example, Joseph refused to lie with Portiphar's wife for he was afraid of sinning against God *(Genesis 39: 7-9).* Daniel and his friends in a foreign land refused to eat food sacrificed to idols even though they were in a privileged selection of youths being trained for royal duties and it was expected of them to partake of these foods. *(Daniel 1:1-21).*

Joseph and Daniel's decisions could be attributed to good and Godly upbringing such that even though their parents were not present, they knew what to do and did just that.

OTHER CHILDREN WHO GREW UP FEARING AND LOVING THE LORD

- Samuel *(1 Samuel 3:1-11).* Eli brought him up. He started hearing God from childhood. Until he died, he was one of the respected prophets in Israel.
- Naaman's maid *(2 Kings 5:2-3).* Captured in a battle, she ended up becoming the maid of Naaman's wife. She told her mistress where Namaan could be healed of leprosy. She was a missionary in the position of a maid.
- Joash *(2Chronicles 24).* He became king at the age of seven. He did what was right before God and got the temple repaired.
- Josiah *(2Chronicles 34).* He became the king at age eight, did what was right before the Lord, got rid of the idols and their altars, cleaned up the land and repaired

the temple. He humbled himself before the Lord and got his people to repent also.
- Rhoda *(Acts 12:13-16).* A servant girl who joined others in praying for the release of Peter. She was the only one that heard Peter's knock but in excitement did not open the door for Peter before running to tell the group.
- Timothy *(2Timothy 1:1-5).* Paul's adopted son/trainee. His mother and grandmother brought him up to fear the Lord. He became a young minister of the gospel.
- Moses *(Hebrews 11:24-25).* Adopted but grew up to be Israel's deliverer from slavery.

YOU NEED WISDOM

No matter what difficulties and problems you are going through, you are the best parent or nurse for the child God has given you. It is not about your background, wealth, affluence, qualification, or experience; it is about the faithful God who has specially assigned you and equipped you for the task.

It is not unusual for God to specially choose a child to rise to fame or wealth above their parents or other siblings. For instance, babies, toddlers or children who get involved in advertisement, movie films, singing or sports to an amazing level, could sometimes earn six figure incomes or more but that still does not remove the fact that they are children and need to be trained and taught in the way of the Lord. Parents, nurses, teachers must not fear them, but in love, nurse and train them still.

As the world becomes more advanced and the devil becomes more sophisticated in his tricks and subtle deceptions to frustrate God's glorious plan for your child, you also should not be ignorant of his devices:

Lest Satan should get an advantage of us: for we are not ignorant of his devices *(2 Corinthians 2:11).*

Always go to God in prayer asking for wisdom to do a good job as a parent *(Matthew 7: 7-10; James 1:5-8).*

WHO ARE YOUR CHILD'S FRIENDS?

Be interested in every aspect of your child's development and growth. Get to know your child's friends and that way God can use you to minister salvation, Godliness and other good virtues to them if they don't have these yet. You might probably get to understand and know your child better through the friends he or she keeps. Check out where your child goes, with whom they move and what they get to do whilst they are with such friends.

Years ago, there was a widow who had two children who were fond of weekly weekend /holiday visits to many Church families. They hardly spent a weekend in their own home. Unknown to their mum, whenever they were away from their home, the children indulged in watching films and videos, which their mother would never have approved of and they picked some bad habits as well. Their mother was not aware until an auntie came to live with them for a short while and found out. This widow was shocked to learn what her children have been allowed to do in other Church members' homes to say the least. Please don't assume that since your child is with a deacon, pastor or Elder's child he or she is safe. You still need to check on him/her.

Teach your child to be 'street wise' lest they become gullible and exposed to wolves out there. Innocent Tamar was a victim of Amnon and his wicked friend, Jonadab's plan. *(2 Samuel 13:1-20)*

WHAT IS YOUR CHILD READING?

The eyes and ears are entrances to the mind, soul, and body. It is therefore important for parents to be mindful of the type of magazine, books, television programmes or movies and music that their child is exposed to. Not too long ago on television, Pastor Benny Hinn was praying for a woman suffering from a terrible cancer. As he prayed, God showed him what was responsible for the cancer: it was a particular occultic book that she had read that Satan used to get access into her. This lady was shocked to learn this and confirmed that truly it was after reading the book that she took ill. She was instructed to go back home and burn the book completely.

WHAT IS YOUR CHILD WATCHING?

There was the story of a young lady who started having demonic manifestations following her watching a particular film in the cinema. Please don't be too busy not to watch the television with your child or go to the movies with him/her, and then you can vet what is being watched and teach informally on things seen if need be. Avoid leaving children to watch television or movies unsupervised. A wise mother of two teenage boys once said that in her home they all watch the same television together not because they cannot conveniently afford other ones for their bedrooms but for her to be able to monitor what her sons are watching. The television was to be switched off once the mother was ready to go to bed. Putting a television in your child's room could open that child to many ungodly lifestyles. More so, such a child may become withdrawn, reserved, go into crime or drugs, become promiscuous or become suicidal, etc. Some children with unsupervised Internet access have ended up in the wrong websites and are now into occultism, pornography, or killed when they have gone to meet with their internet friend etc.

RIGHT TIMING

Ecclesiastes chapter 3 verse 1 says there is a time for everything yet many Christians are not spiritually alert enough to recognise a subtle distraction of the enemy. Pharaoh was against the Israelites going to worship God with their children and the world still has that same attitude today. It is gradually becoming the norm in many societies today that extra curricular or club activities in schools are scheduled not only for Sundays but also at the very same time that the worship service is going on in the Church. Unfortunately many Christian parents want their children to excel in these activities and so allow their children to go for dancing, football or other sports instead of going to Church.

Whilst this may be acceptable once in a while, parents should ensure that the child attends the mid-week service or teaching when he or she has to be away from the Sunday service. It is time for Christian parents to affirm like Moses, 'we will go and worship the Lord with our children' and like Joshua, be able to declare that 'as for me and my house we will serve the Lord.'

BE AWARE OF UNGODLY DECREES

It is a known truth that to get the best out of any equipment or product, the maker's manual is to be followed. What is true for the physical is true for the spiritual. Christian parents need to rise up from slumber and be involved in making sure that decrees and legislations are not set up to destroy our children, physically or spiritually especially in terms of their education, health, love and honour of God. We are their voices and God is depending on us. Christian parents must be actively involved in the activities that concern where they reside or work and importantly in the children's schools. We need to read the prints and in-between the prints avoiding all of Pharaoh's negotiations *(Exodus 8;10)*.

For example, any legislation that aims at teaching Christian children that homosexuality or transsexuality is alright is ungodly *(Leviticus18:22-30; 20:13-16)*.

A legislation that makes it right to hand condoms, morning after pills etc. to children without parental knowledge or consent is surely ungodly. The Bible condemns sexual intercourse outside marriage for God knows that there is nothing such as 'safe sex' outside of marriage. The fact that our society tolerates and encourages it does not make it godly or right. It is possible with God's help to keep one's virginity until married even today. Christian parents need to teach and address the issue of sexual intercourse in line with the word of God. Any legislation that campaigns for 'safe sex' instead of 'no sex or abstinence' outside of marriage is an ungodly decree.

The Bible says that foolishness is bound in the heart of a child; but the rod of correction shall drive it far from him *(Proverbs 22:15)*. In another chapter it says, to discipline and reprimand a child produces wisdom, but a mother is disgraced by an undisciplined child *(Proverbs 29:15)*. It follows then that a legislation that prevents Christian parents from teaching and training their children is ungodly. Christian parents should however always distinguish between discipline and abuse. Discipline done in love brings correction and knowledge to the child whilst abuse brings trauma. Parents are to discipline and not abuse children. The Bible instructs parents to love, teach, train and discipline their children, not maltreat them *(Proverbs 13:24; 22:6; 23:13-14)*.

TEACH BY EXAMPLE

A write up from the Daily Bread of October 7, 1994 reads: 'A child may not inherit his/her parent's talents but he/she will absorb their values. A child takes with him/her the behaviour and value system modelled by the parents thus the greatest gift a parent can give you is a worthy example. Whatever you write on the heart of a child, is written indelibly there. Each action and word makes an impact you know like a kindness or a beautiful prayer.'

WHY NURSE CHILDREN FOR THE LORD?

- God commands it *(Deuteronomy 6:4-9, Genesis 18:18-19)*
- In God's agenda for the world, every child matters *(Psalm 139:13–18; Jeremiah 1:4-5).*
- Children are lost in sin *(Romans 3:23; 6:23).*
- God loves them so must we *(John 3:16-17; Mark 10; Matthew 18:5)*
- God's wish is for them not to perish *(Matthew 18:14)*
- Children have long been neglected – the Holy Spirit is able to teach them and open their understanding to the things of God.
- Children are easily exposed to the wolves of demonic operations – occult activities, immorality in the media, etc.
- Children are humble and have teachable hearts *(Matthew 18:3)*
- Great potential lies in them *(Psalm 127:4; Psalm 128:3b).*

- They can believe in Christ and live godly lives (Matthew *18:6).*
- Finally, they are the leaders of tomorrow – our children are born to win, lead and rule. Building them up is building the nation *(Genesis 1:27-28).*

© *Children's Evangelism Ministry, 'Basic Course on Child Evangelism'*

GOD IS WATCHING

Many of today's parents with due respect to them, cannot list the Ten Commandments written in *Exodus 20: 1-17* or recite any of the Psalms. What they don't know or have they cannot give or teach to their spiritually hungry and searching children.

You can only give to your child what you have. If Jesus is not your Lord and Master and you are not following Him daily, how do you intend to nurture that child for God? First, you need to give your life to Jesus and experience His forgiveness, love and mercy. Secondly, you must daily depend on God for guidance. He, who has chosen you to nurse that child, is well able to equip you for the task if only you will go to Him in prayer asking for wisdom to do a good job.

You Need Wisdom

Please love your children, spend time with them, be their parent, friend and confidant. Remember that God has given them to you to nurse for Him.

God does not sleep nor slumber, He watches over every child and He is also watching how faithful you are as a parent. He equally watches the professional and Sunday school teachers for what and how they teach the children in their care. You may justify your actions but God looks at your motive and He will reward you according to your deeds.

Perhaps you have not given your life to Jesus Christ before or you were once a Christian but you are now far away from God and will like to give or rededicate your life to Him, please pause and meaningfully say this prayer with me:

Dear Lord, I am very grateful to You for allowing me to read this book. I realise I am a sinner and I confess all my sins, past, present and future (please list as many as you remember). I come to you just as I am in need of a Saviour, please Lord forgive me for all my sins and cleanse me from all my iniquities. With my heart I believe that Jesus Christ came to this world and died for all my sins, that He rose from the dead and that one day He will come back again. With my mouth I acknowledge my sins and confess them. From now on please be my God, live and dwell in me and teach me all that I need to know about You Lord. Help me to know how best to teach and train our children for You Lord in Jesus name, Thank You Lord for answering my prayers in Jesus' name. I pray with thanksgiving. Amen.

GOOD AND BAD PARENTING

Raising children is a God-assigned task for parents, teachers, government, church and society. It involves much more than bringing them into life, giving them food, clothes, shoes, education, toys, recreation and holidays. Right from infancy, children need to be told about the love of God and His attributes so that they can later on take their rightful place in the Church, home and society.

Train up a child in the way he should go: and when he is old, he will not depart from it. *Proverbs 22:6.*

The Sunday school in particular should do more than keep children quiet, much more than make them sing and watch video tapes etc. It ought to be a time and place of knowing the Lord and fellowshipping with Him even from a tender age. Children need to be taught the word of God in a way that is applicable to their lives at home, school and in the community.

THE REWARDS OF NURTURING CHILDREN FOR THE LORD

Believe it or not God is taking note of our input into these delicate, precious lives and He rewards each person according to how well this task is performed. Children themselves may not necessarily say thank you at first but many often do so later in life when they remember how your love, correction, discipline, teachings, and advice have positively shaped their lives.

THEY WILL NOT DEPART FROM THE LORD

Even when they stray away, they will return to the Lord *(Proverbs 22:6; Luke 15:11-32)*. Under the influence of bad friends and peer pressure, it is not uncommon for children from Christian homes to stray away particularly when they get to higher institutions. However, with prayers of intercession and unconditional love, these youngsters, like the prodigal son, usually return home and to the faith of their parents.

PEACE FOR PARENTS

Parents who have trained their children to always fear God are not afraid of their children coming to destruction so they live in peace. *(Proverbs 19:18; Proverbs 23:24-25; 29:17)*
Many years ago in a particular town, a cinema was engulfed in fire on a Sunday morning. A concerned person immediately informed one woman whose child was schooling in that town. On hearing the time and location of the fire accident, the mother confidently said she was sure her son would not be involved. When asked why she was so sure, she said it was service time on the day of the Lord and she had brought up her son to always be in the service at that time. Indeed what this mother said of her son was later confirmed to be true.

As a parent do you go to bed in fear of a police visit to tell you some bad news about your child's misdeeds or do you have peace knowing that because of the Godly training you have given and with God's help, your child will not choose the pathway of destruction?

GENERATIONAL IMPACT

Consciously or unconsciously, many things are passed from

one generation to the other *(Genesis 18:17-19; Deuteronomy 6:4-9)*. Many who have had a good upbringing will try to give their children an equally good if not better upbringing. Every wise and good parent will strive to teach and lead their children into the secret of their own success and the children in turn will pass it on to future generations.

EXAMPLES OF CHILDREN NOT NURSED FOR THE LORD

- Lot's daughters *(Genesis 19:30-38)*: Lot's relationship with God was not convincing enough for his daughters so they behaved like their neighbours in Sodom and Gomorrah. Instead of trusting God for husbands, they got their father drunk and lay with him to get pregnant.

- Eli's sons *(1Samuel 2:21-25)*: Unlike their father, Eli's sons did not fear God or respect His ordinances. They slept with women in the temple and took meat from the offerings people brought to the Lord before the sacrifices were completed. God rejected them from becoming priests after Eli and allowed both sons to be killed in battle on the same day.

- Samuel's children *(1 Samuel 8:1-6)*: They also did not

walk in the way of their father Samuel so much so that the people rejected them being their leaders when Samuel became old. Their unremarkable behaviour made the Israelites ask Samuel for a king like other nations around them.

- Amnon *(2 Samuel 13: 1-39)*.: he raped his half sister Tamar committing incest and that invariably led to his murder by assassins organised by one of his half brothers sometime later.

- Absalom *(2 Samuel 15)*: King David's son Absolom was a handsome young man with very long hair. His father neither trained nor disciplined him. Absalom killed his half brother for raping his sister. He burnt Joab's farm and harvest in protest. He conspired against David and proclaimed himself king whilst David was very much alive, making his father flee for safety. He slept with his father's concubine on the rooftop – publicly. Finally, he got killed in a battle against King David.

- Rehoboam: Solomon's son *(1 Kings 12:1-24)*. Out of lack of good training and disobedience to the elders who advised his father, he gave a harsh reply to the demands of the people and he lost his throne.

Untrained children will always lose the family inheritance

because they lack wisdom and have no sense of appreciation.

From the above examples, we can see that bad parenting usaully leads to death of the child, physically, emotionally and spiritually. If care is not taken it can also lead to untold sorrow and death of the parent *(1Samuel 3: 11-14; 4:1-18; Proverbs 15:20; 10:1; 29:15).* Bad parents are sure to suffer destruction and divine punishment *(Matthew 18:6).*
Parental discipline that is given too late leads to heartbreak while parental discipline that is never given leads to heartbreak and a neck break.

In conclusion, I would like to share with you two articles and a poem that I read recently. I have modified the first one to read "A Parent's Prayer".

A PARENT'S PRAYER

Lord, can you forgive me for hurting my children? I came from poverty, so I thought a big house would make my children feel important. I didn't realise that all it takes is – my love. I thought money would bring them happiness; all it did was to make them think that things were more important than people.

I thought spanking them would make them tough, so they could defend themselves; all it did was stop me from seeking wisdom so that I could discipline and teach them. I thought that leaving them alone would make them independent; all it did was force my first-born to be a father to my second son. I thought by 'smoothing over' family problems I was keeping peace. All I was teaching them was run rather than lead.

I thought that by pretending to be the perfect family, I was bringing them up respectably; all I was teaching them was to live a lie and keep a secret. I thought that all I had to do to be their parent was make money and supply their material needs; all I taught them was that there is more to being a parent. The problem is – now they have to guess what being a parent really is.

PS: Dear God, I hope you can read this prayer. My tears have smudged a lot of the words.

John Ellis, The Word for Today. May 21 1999

I have modified and re-arranged this poem by Amanda Cater:

If a child lives with approval –s/he learns to like her/himself
If a child lives with criticism – s/he learns to condemn

If a child lives with encouragement – s/he learns confidence
If a child lives with fairness – s/he learns justice
If a child lives with hostility – s/he learns to fight
If a child lives with praise – s/he learns to appreciate
If a child lives with ridicule –s/he learns to be shy
If a child lives with security – s/he learns to have faith
If a child lives with shame – s/he learns to be guilty
If a child lives with tolerance - s/he learns to be patient
If a child lives with acceptance and friendship
S/he learns to find love both in her/himself and in the world.

Source: http://www.poemhunter.com/poem/if-a-child/.

The second article is entitled, Ten Commandments for Parents.

TEN COMMANDMENTS FOR PARENTS

- My hands are small: don't expect perfection whenever I make a bed, draw a picture or throw a ball. My legs are short. Slow down so that I can keep up with you.
- My eyes have not seen the world as yours have. Let me explore it safely; don't restrict me unnecessarily.
- Make time for me. Housework will always be there; I'm little only once.
- I have feelings too; don't nag me about my inquisitiveness. Treat me as you'd like to be treated.
- I'm a gift; treasure me as God intended. Hold me

accountable, give me guidelines to live by, discipline me with love.
- I need encouragement to grow, not empty praise. Go easy you can correct the things I do without putting me down.
- Give me the freedom to make decisions, even if they're not always right. Permit me to fall, so that I can learn to walk.
- Don't do things repeatedly for me; that make me feel like my efforts don't measure up to your expectations. And don't compare me with others; I'm me, not them.
- Don't be afraid to leave for a weekend together. Kids need time away from parents, just like parents need it from kids. Besides, it shows us that your marriage is something special.
- Take me to God's house and introduce me to Him, because I'll need Him for the rest of my life.
©*Word for Today 2000*

I encourage every parent to write out these 10 commandments on a card and place it somewhere you can read it every day.

It is time for you as a parent to discover or re-discover your child. A wise person once said that the time spent with your child plus commitment plus interest equals love.

Every child is born to win and born to lead. In the name

of Jesus Christ, I challenge you to take your children and nurse them for the Lord and He will give you your wages.

If you are ready to take up the challenge, please say this prayer:

> *Dear Father, thank you for helping me to read and understand this book. I realise the great privilege and opportunity of being a parent, guardian and or teacher. Thank you Lord for my children, _____ (mention their names), the treasure(s) that you have entrusted in my care.*
>
> *Father, please I need your help in the following areas of my child's development (put his/her/their names and needs). Lord in line with your word; please grant me all that will help me to successfully raise my children in Your way. In Jesus name I have prayed with thanksgiving. Amen.*

POEMS

GOD'S GIFT YOU CAN NEVER BUY

Friend, have you ever thought about something?
I mean about God's numerous gifts to mankind?
Isn't God wonderful and generous to you and me?
All His gifts to mankind, He gave free of charge.

Beginning with life itself, it is free to mankind
Money can buy good medicine and care but not life or health
The air we breathe in is abundant and free
Can you imagine if we have to pay for that in a day?

Nothing quenches thirst as much as ordinary water
Yet in abundance, God has made it available to man
The radiant sun breaks the dawn and shines bright
All living things depend on it for their growth and vitality.

That pretty baby is a wonderful gift from God
Medicine can help produce test tube babies
Yet the sperm and egg are really God's
Indeed God's gift you and I can never buy.

Imagine Jesus having to pay the heavy price for our sins
On the cross, He was hanged for you and me
Shedding His innocent and sinless blood
For there is none else qualified for the atonement required.

What on earth is equivalent to the shed blood?
What can we pay for such an eternal sacrifice?
Who among the prophets could stand in the gap?
To appease God's wrath and justice against man?

Tell me which power is equal to that of the Holy Spirit
Who is as humble and powerful as Him?
Yet at Pentecost, He was poured on the disciples
And today, He is still empowering Christians.

Simon the sorcerer thought he could buy salvation
And possibly a bit of the Holy Ghost manifestations
He asked the apostles for it, offering some money
How he must have thought such gift can be bought?

Haven't we in previous times tried to buy some of God's gifts?
By the very way we think and live our lives
Why not pause and think when next you are tempted
There is no controversy, God's gift you can never buy.

There are not enough riches in the world, the Bible says
To redeem just a single soul from hell fire
There are not enough blankets or scientific discoveries
To cover the glory of the most tiny star in the sky.

Indeed God's gift you can never buy.

© O.Ola-Ojo. 1992 Genesis 1:1-end.

TOUCH SOMEONE TODAY

There are five senses in a human being
The sense of sight, hearing and smell
That of tasting and touching
Through which messages are received and relayed.

However, the power of touching is so real
Whilst others could easily be mistaken or unnoticed
That of touch cannot be mistaken or easily forgotten
Especially in times of great needs of man.

No wonder the Rabbi begged Jesus for a touch
On His little daughter who had just died at home
Great was his faith in Jesus' healing power
That would raise the dead girl just by a mere touch.

The unnamed woman with the issue of blood
Had suffered for twelve years in the hands of all
Despised, rejected, weak, feeble, faint and weary
She sought for complete healing from Jesus Christ.

Aware of all the difficulties to be encountered
She was contented only with touching Jesus' garment
For she believed that would procure the desired healing
What a joy as her faith was honoured and recognised.

'Stir up the gift of God' Paul admonished Timothy,
Which had been given to you when hands were laid
Upon your head, and be no longer afraid of anything
But filled with power, love and a strong mind.

Stop underestimating that touch of the Almighty God
Upon you dear friend through God's messengers
Begin today to flow in God's mighty power
Unto every being you come in contact with.

Be kind to give a friendly touch dear friend
To that person you know needs your help now
To that very sick child and the worried parent
Let them feel God's love and power through your touch.

God is able to bring about the miracle through you
Identify with that person's problem today
As you reach out to touch him/her and the need
If anything, dear friend touch someone today.

© O. Ola-Ojo 8/7/90.

DESPISE THEM NOT

There is the human tendency of looking down on others
Especially the less privileged ones amongst us
The Lord strictly warns you and I in the Bible
Not to despise these weak and unfortunate ones.

'Despise not the children' Jesus once told the disciples
'For to them belongs the kingdom of heaven'
'In heaven their angels always behold the face of God'
What more, God is interested in them as much as you.

Despise not the widows, orphans or widowers
For their redeemer is strong and He will defend them
Never rob or injure the sick people too
For the Lord is their defender and He will punish you.

Despise not the poor neither should you mock them
Or cheat them because of their poverty, the scripture warns
For a curse is upon those who close their eyes to their needs
Whilst God will supply the needs of those who help them.

Despise them not whatever their condition or handicap
For before God we are all the same, the handicap not withstanding
Your own soul is destroyed when you are cruel
And it is nourished when you are kind to others.

© O. Ola-Ojo 29/04/89 and 18/05/89

Matthew. 18:10,19:13-14, Proverbs.11: 17,23:11,19:22,14:21,31, 17:5

Proverbs 19:17, 24:23, 28:27, and 29:13

NOBODY EVER KNOWS

God in His mercies calls people over and over
At various times, in various places over and over
For various purposes in His own perfect timetable
Nobody ever knows the extent of such calling
Nobody ever knows the demands of such calling
Nobody ever knows the degree of problems to be expected
Nobody ever knows the opportunities and privileges.

Abram was called out of his hometown
To an unknown land where God was to lead him
Leaving his people with members of his family
Never to return again to the land nor his friends
Never to allow his son Isaac to go there for a visit
Only to have his faith tested for twenty-five years
Never realised he was to later be the father of all nations.

Moses the stammerer was chosen to lead the people
Out of bondage in Egypt to the Promised Land
He did not appreciate his capability of doing so
Nor did he realise that God had noticed his humility
He never knew of the test awaiting him at the Red sea
He never envisaged manna from heaven and water from the rock
He never knew these would make him become a friend of God.

At the time Saul of Tarsus personally met the Lord
Little did he realise the great heavenly mission afore him
Neither did he know he was to face serious persecutions
Nor become a prisoner, he who was of the Jewish blood
Nor did he realise how many letters he would write in prison
Anointed admonitions, challenges and encouragement to all people
That will be very useful and meaningful up till now.

My brother, my beloved sister, nobody ever knows
Why God has called you, even you, for that great assignment
You may not know how to begin and go about the assignment
You may not know what it is all about and what it entails
You may not know what blessings await mankind out of it
You may not know how rewarding it will be for you in the end
His plans will daily be unfolded as you yield to the Holy Spirit.

© O. Ola-Ojo 22/10/90. Based on Proverbs 20:24

WHY THE STIGMA?

At creation God looked at everything He had created
And pronounced them good in His sight
Man and woman were to be fruitful and multiply
Subduing all the earth the maker commanded them.

The entrance of sin led to sickness and death
Some of which have continued in families over the years
Many children today are born with congenital diseases
Of which they are innocent yet made the scapegoat,

Such unfortunate children grow to suffer most times
In the hands of ignorant members of their family
In the hands of unsympathetic, unloving hospital workers
In the hands of a government who is very least concerned.

Some of such people have been deprived of a good living
The social stigma attached to them has caused untold heartache
The spiritual stigma sometimes has driven them from the Lord.
The economic stigma has reduced their lifespan and its quality.

Suffering begins when the child cannot act or plays like his age mates
When he has to be kept away from certain places and plays
When he has to be restricted or curtailed in many ways and times
When he is given the impression of being too sickly and unwanted.

At school the teacher expects too much from him
Mates avoid him for they believe his sickness is infectious
He is denied and deprived of many opportunities and goods
Many times no one is interested in his God given abilities or gifts

After graduation to get a job becomes more difficult
He is turned down not because of his inability but for his ailment
The society still refuses to give him their support
No wonder many of such people become depressed or introverts.

The poor individual sometimes loses his personal name
The society would rather call him by his ailment or disability
They give him a stigma name without thinking twice
No one cares what negative effect this will have on his personality.

Such was the case of the woman with the issue of blood
For twelve years the law of the land curtailed her
No association with the public whom she would defile
Not even to be allowed into the temple where she could seek God's face.

The ten lepers were barred from the community where they
were born
Outside the camp they were destined to live forever
Not knowing the salvation of the community depended on them
As they were the ones who later brought the wonderful news.

To the person who has been stigmatised I suggest
That you draw closer to Jesus the only faithful friend
He alone is capable of removing that stigma today
He alone can help you to live above your difficulties.

To the members of His family may I appeal?
That you show more positive love and understanding
God doesn't punish people. He loves people
Even those with that known physical ailment.

To the medical staff and the general public
Let us prayerfully change that unloving attitude
To the government of the land I appeal in the name of the Lord
That you show genuine concern for these stigmatised ones as well.

© O. Ola-Ojo 1991. Based on 2Kings 7:3-10

& Luke 8:43-48

I LOVED THEM BOTH DEARLY

Mine were the two boys, both from my loins
The younger was somewhat lazy and inconsiderate
Not too keen on the work on the farms
Selfish often in his thinking and actions
But I loved him dearly.

Once he came to make a request of me
That of having his inheritance whilst I was alive
He couldn't wait for me to pass on to glory
Selfishly he demanded his right at the wrong time
But I loved him still.

I gave him his inheritance and to a far country he went
Not telling me where he was off to and for how long
Not minding what torments his request had on us
To me, his mother, brother, family and friends
But I loved him still.

I was heartbroken when he left
I did not stop him travelling even though I could
I allowed him to go for a lifetime adventure
I believed and prayed he will come back home
But I loved him dearly.

Everyday I watched out for his coming home
No one seemed to have a clue where he was
No one told me of what sort of life he was living
No one but I kept on watching out for him
For I loved him still.

One ordinary day I saw someone coming up our path
Ragged, weary, worn out and in shame he came
Apologising for his past mistakes to God and to me
Asking that he be considered for a servant position
But I loved him even more.

I embraced him in love and wept over him
Prayers answered and dreams come to pass
I ordered that he be clothed in new garments
A ring for his finger and shoes for his weary feet
But I loved him still.

I ordered that the fattened calf be killed
It was time for a huge family celebration
My younger son's return was worth it all
A time to publicly restore him to his sonship position
Now I loved him best.

My older son very obedient and hardworking
Unlike his brother never asking hardly daring
He was always by my side come rain come sunshine
He was on the farm when his younger brother arrived
I loved him very much too.

All these years he has been by my side working
He had watched my character and attitude day and night
I longed for him to at least be like me in his attitude
Alas he refused to come into the party because of anger
But I loved him too.

I went out to meet him and asked him why he was angry
He told me I had never given him a kid to celebrate with his friends
He judged his younger brother's lifestyle abroad without seeing him
He seemed not to care whether his younger brother lived or died.
But I loved him more.

All I have is yours son I told him to his amazement
You did not have because you did not ask me for anything
The blood of the calf has been shed in the party for you and your brother
The party is only for those who would come just as they were
But I loved him too very much.

Mine were the two boys both from my loins
Different in character, attitude and traits
Same parents, same upbringing, same environment
Different in what was in their minds and life goals
But I loved them both and equally too.

© O.Ola – Ojo 22/08/04 Luke 15: 11-32

TRAIN THEM OR LOSE THEM.

I was the high priest for my generation
I was serving God and His people
As best as I knew, I served day and night
Blessed with two sons, a happy man I was

I thought they would follow in all my steps
Fearing the Lord and serving Him and the people
They knew all about the priestly procedures I felt
Until reports started getting to me of their behaviour

A prophet came and warned me about my sons
I called them and told them off for their bad actions
Little Samuel also had a vision from God
My boys after all were not as trained as I had thought

Too late to train them I thought so I warned them
I was too busy with God's assignment and the people
I had little Samuel to bring up in the way of the Lord
In the end I left the situation not doing much to change it.

Train them or lose them I kept hearing over and over again
How do I now train my matured, greedy, God fearless sons?
Then came an unexpected war with the Philistines our enemies
In the same day both sons and one of my daughters-in-law died.

© O.Ola – Ojo 22/08/04 based on 1 Samuel 3: 10-21, 4:1-21.

WHERE ARE THE GOOD FATHERS TODAY?

Where are the good fathers today?
That is the heart cry of the mothers
That is the desperate plea of the children
That is the great missing link in our society
Where are the good fathers today?

Where are the good fathers today?
Fathers who live in the fear of God
Fathers who lead children by their example
Fathers who are the priests in the home
Where are the good fathers today?

Where are the good fathers today?
Fathers who are not children molesters
Fathers who are not wife abusers
Fathers who do not unleash terror
Where are the good fathers today?

Where are the good fathers today?
Fathers who teach sense and sensibility
Fathers who teach the fear and love of God
Fathers who teach love and respect for life
Where are the good fathers today?

Where are the good fathers today?
Fathers who command respect
Fathers who don't seek to dominate others
Fathers who walk in God's authority
Where are the good fathers today?

Where are the good fathers today?
Fathers who walk in the truth of God's word
Fathers who talk with God's authority
Fathers who speak only the mind of God
Where are the good fathers today?

Where are the good fathers today?
Fathers who teach from their scars
Fathers who will not use birthmarks as an excuse
Fathers who will teach every aspect of life
Where are the good fathers today?

Where are the good fathers today?
Fathers who celebrate each of their children
Fathers who celebrate each child's development
From smiling to sitting, crawling to passing examinations
Where are the good fathers today I dare to ask you?

© O. Ola-Ojo November 2004.

OPPORTUNITY TO BECOME A CHRISTIAN

Dear Father in heaven,

Thank you for the privilege of reading this book. 'Indeed I have sinned and come short of Your glory.' I am grateful to You for sending Jesus Christ into this world to come to die on the cross of Calvary for me. I believe in my heart that Jesus Christ paid for my sins, past, present and future. I believe Jesus Christ was buried and on the third day He rose from the dead. I believe that Jesus Christ will come back again. I confess with my mouth and I accept Him now to be my Lord.

Master, Saviour, Brother, and Friend. I ask in Your mercy for the infilling of the Holy Spirit so that with His help, I can live a victorious life becoming all that You have ordained me to be in Jesus' name I pray with thanksgiving. Amen.

If after reading this book you said the above prayer and became bornagain, 'Congratulations! You are Born Again' is a booklet for those who have done so through reading this book. It is a free booklet that we would like you to have. In it, the frequently asked questions are answered and this will get you on the way to growing in your newfound faith in God. You can download this free booklet from our website: www.protokospublishers.com

You may also contact any of the organisations listed at the end of the book.

I look forward to hearing from you soon.
O. Ola–Ojo

Other Books By The Author:

Provocation, Prayer and Praise
(December 2004 & 2009)

Complimentary to The Christian and Infertility this book focuses on the story of an infertile woman in the Bible, her provocations, prayer and praise. Whatever makes you incomplete, unfulfilled, less than whom God made you to be, whatever issue of life that the enemy uses to provoke you calls for prayer.

Key features include:
- Some known medical reasons for infertility in the women.
- Why Hannah went to the house of God in spite of her barrenness.
- Is it true that the husband is much more than 10 sons to the infertile woman?
- When, where and how to address the source/cause of your provocation.
- God's part and your part in that promise.
- God is able to met that humanly impossible need of yours.
- A time to celebrate and praise God.

Book Details:
Paperback: 128 pages
Language English
ISBN-13: 978-0-9557898-3-0

A Reader from London, 7 Jan 2006 on Amazon.co.uk
An excellent easy to read and understand book. The principles shared in this book though primarily are for those trying for a baby could as well be applied to any area of hurt and un-fulfilment.

 :www.protokospublishers.com

The Christian and Infertility
(December 2004 & 2009)

The Christian and Infertility addresses one of the often neglected needs of Christian couples. It gives an insight into infertility from the biblical and medical perspectives. It is written not only for potential fruitful couples but for pastors, family and friends of these couples. It is written that the Body of Christ might be fully equipped to know and support couples who are facing the challenge of infertility at present.

Key features include:
- Childleness in the Bible and lessons to learn;
- Some possible physical, medical and environmental causes of infertility;
- Some known spiritual causes of infertility;
- The man and low sperm count;
- Some of the available treatment optons in the UK;
- Choice of fertility treatment;
- Should a christian professional be involved in fertility treatment?

Book Details:
Paperback: 146 pages
Language English
ISBN-13: 978-0-9557898-2-3

A reviewer from Glen Burnie, USA, 29 Oct 2007 on Amazon.co.uk'
The book is a great eye-opener for all. It sheds light on infertility from the medical and spiritual angle. This gives the reader a balance because i believe every human being is made up of both physical and spiritual part. To get a balance in life, the two parts must be well fed. One must not concentrate on the spiritual and neglect the physical part. The book also reminds us that God has a way of sorting us out.... The book is quite inspiring. I will recommend this book to everybody trusting God for any form of blessing from God to go get one and apply it to his or her situation. It will definitely bless you and yours'.

 :www.protokospublishers.com

Obstetrics and Gynaecology Ultrasound - A Self-Assessment Guide

June 2005 Churchill Elsevier Publishers, UK.

This self-assessment guide is a structured questions and answer book that develops the reader's understanding capability using a simple method in treating related topics. Clinical indications are presented with their corresponding ultrasound findings using appropriate illustrations. A case study approach is followed; presenting the clinical and ethical dilemmas that might arise whilst encouraging students to think. The aim is to reinforce theoretical knowledge within a clinical environment.

Key features:
- Over 600 high-resolution ultrasound images
- Cover a wide spectrum of ultrasound curriculum.
- Includes a detailed study of fertility.
- Aids quick understanding of subject matter.
- 468 pages.

ISBN-10: 0443064628
ISBN-13: 978-0443064623
Book Dimensions: 24 x 16.8 x 2.6 cm

"...*This excellent new book is a study guide... This is an attractive paperback that should be essential reading for trainee obstetric and gynaecological sonographers, whether they are radiographers or radiology or obstetric trainees. It will be of particular value to those preparing for the RCOG/RCR Diploma in Advanced Obstetric Ultrasound and to specialist registrars in obstetrics and gynaecology undertaking special skills modules in fetal medicine, gynaecological ultrasound and infertility...*"

The Obstetrician & Gynaecologist, www.rcog.org.uk/togonline
Book reviews 2006

Reviewer **Ann Harper MD FRCPI FRCOG.**
Consultant Obstetrician and Gynaecologist
Royal Jubilee Maternity Service, Belfast., UK

 :www.protokospublishers.com

There is a Reward for Parenting.

GOOD MUMS, BAD MUMS
(June 2005 & 2009)

This is in two parts, the main chapter that can be used for personal or group study, and an accompanying exercise section. The privileged position of a mother is in her being a co-creator with God and bringing forth life (lives). This book compliments one of God's previous revelations to me as contained in the book titled Good Dads, Bad Dads'. While the father could be likened to the pilot of the family plane, the mother can be likened to the force behind the plane – positive or negative. Good mothers are not only co-creators with God, they also do nurture as well as nourish their children physically, emotionally and spiritually.

Keys Features:
- Were all the mothers in the Bible god mothers?
- Lessons from the strengths and weakness of seven mothers.
- Be encouraged - you are not alone in the assignment of motherhood.
- Be motivated in the areas of your strengths.
- Learn ways of supporting your husband and children.

Book Details:
Paperback: 162 pages
Language English
ISBN-13: 978-0-9557898-1-6
Book Dimensions: 21.4 x 14 x 1.4 cm

I appreciate the author's method of writing. It is always exciting holding her book to read. Personally, 'Good Mums, Bad Mums' has been a blessing to me in no small measure. The book is rich, it is loaded with physical and spiritual uplifting subjects. To all existing and potential mothers, this book is a MUST read. At the end of every chapter there is an exercise to do that will help in re-examining your life spiritually and in other ways. I encourage all women to get and use this book as a guide in raising their children. You will be glad you did.

Pastor Mrs T Adegoke
Freedom Arena
London, UK

 :www.protokospublishers.com

To the Bride with Love
(2007 & 2009)

Every wise woman preparing to get married knows she will need sound advice, practical tips and solid, heartfelt prayers, of those who have travelled on the road she is about to journey on. In this book, 10 women of different age groups, from different backgrounds and cultures who wedded under various circumstances, individually share their experience with the bride in an intimate, very candid and unforgettable way.

Book details:
Paperback: 108 pages
Language English
ISBN-13: 978-0-9557898-4-7
Book Dimensions: 22.4 x 15 x 1 cm

To the Bride with Love is the perfect bride's evergreen companion. The content is suitable, relevant and applicable even decades after the wedding day.
To the Bride with Love is an ideal wedding gift on its own. It can also accompany any other gift (big or small) that you have for the bride but take this hint… the bride will keep thanking you for the book years and years after.

'One of the best', 19 Jul 2008 on Amazon.com
Sade Olaoye "clare4good" (United Kingdom)
This book has really helped my marriage from the onset as I got it as a wedding gift, God bless the giver. It's a must read fro relationship improvement and God's guidance. I recommend people to get for oneself and also as a great blessing for someone else in love. "To the Bride with Love"

Review by Oyinlola Odunlami CEO.
Shallom Bookshop, London UK

The writing style of Oluwakemi is unique, peculiar and distinct to herself. I recommend To the Bride with Love to wives, wives to be, mothers, mentors, youth leaders and workers. Why? The clarity, the focus and the intent of this book is so empowering, encouraging and enlightening

There is a Reward for Parenting.

that it will definitely mould or re mould a life to achieve its purpose. The truth is, there are very few books that have depth as well as help you to achieve your goals and arrive at your destination. Many books tend to excite you but have no depth; you read and you forget; they do not really change you but this book, To the Bride with Love will definitely leave a word in your spirit and move you to your next level!

I believe that this is also a book that pastors will find useful as a manual for marriage counselling, because many books on marriage focus mostly on what you as an individual can gain, your own personal satisfaction while little is said about the sacrifices involved and their importance. As my pastor usually says, it is important to learn from those who have gone ahead, understand why some were successful and others weren't, so that we won't fall where they fell, rather, we would gain more speed, achieve our goals and thereby glorify Christ.

So, I invite you not only to get a copy of this life-changing manual for yourself, but also to put it into as many hands as you can afford to, for then the world will definitely benefit and your life will be a blessing to many.

:www.protokospublishers.com

Refuge Under His Wings

"an exhaustive analysis of the Book of Ruth in the Bible. The author combines her deep Christian conviction and excellent knowledge of the Holy Scriptures to produce a must read for every Christian, married or single. The book is interspaced with beautifully written prayers, which enables the reader to pause, pray and meditate on the revelations received... The book is also loaded with poetry like 'Thy will be done oh Lord' for those who may be facing an uncertain future or on a cross road of decisions."

Dr E B Ekpo MD, FRCP
Queen Elizabeth Hospital, Christian Fellowship,
Woolwich, London. UK

"...[a] ...spiritually sound book... a fine work of thoughtful reading and study... I therefore recommend it to every Christian, married or single....
Pat Roach Senior Pastor
New Covenant Church.
Wandsworth Branch, London. UK.

Book details:
Paperback: 100 pages
Language English
ISBN-10: 095578980X
ISBN-13: 978-0955789809

This book feeds the soul. Most of all I loved the poetry. It gives you time to savour the thoughts as reader. There is a good mix of poetry and prose.To look at the story of Ruth in depth gave good spiritual food. You can pause and take it in at your own pace.The meditation on Psalm 121 was good also. There's nothing like reading a Psalm slowly and meditating on its contents. The author's own reflections allow you to see the book through someone else's eyes. A good read.

Book Review: by **Gaby Richards**, London, UK.

 :www.protokospublishers.com

GRACE OR WORKS

This book makes you examine a lot of issues in your life, family relationships in particular, that you may have taken for granted or totally ignored. As conveyed right from the rhetorical question posed in the title, Grace or Works, the author stirs you towards asking yourself pertinent questions, thinking through for answers and even getting solutions for unresolved problems.

Have you heard of prodigal wives, husbands, mothers or prodigal fathers? This book identifies and defines them clearly. For anyone experiencing a crises in their relationship with such prodigal family members, this book, which is based on the parable of the "Prodigal son" in Luke 15:11-32 is a one-stop resource material to meet your counselling needs. And just in case you happen to be the prodigal who has caused your relatives much sorrow, there is hope for you in this book.

Interspersed with prayers for you by the author and specific prayers that you can say for yourself, as well as poems to comfort and inspire you, Grace or Works not only asks you questions, it helps you make and maintain the right choices.

Book details:
Paperback: 122 pages
Language English
ISBN-13: 978-0-9557898-5-4

 :www.protokospublishers.com

COMING OUT SOON

- GOOD DADS, BAD DADS.
- INSPIRATIONS FOR THE MAN OF VALOUR.
- INSPIRATIONS FOR THE MAN OF COURAGE.
- LET'S REASON TOGETHER - YOUTH'S A-Z.

USEFUL ADDRESSES & WEBSITES

Care for the Family
PO Box 488
Cardiff
CF15 7YY
Tel: (029) 2081 0800
Fax: (029) 2081 4089
Email: mail@cff.org.uk
Website: www.care-for-the-family.org.uk OR www.cff.org.uk
Care for the Family aims to promote strong family life and to help those hurting because of family breakdown. Their heart is to come alongside people in the good times and in the tough times – bringing hope, compassion and some practical, down-to-earth help and encouragement.

Children Evangelism Ministry Inc
P.O. Box 4480
Ilorin, Kwara State,
Nigeria.
Tel: +234 31 222199
E-mail: cem@ilorin.skannet.com OR cem562000@yahoo.com
Children Evangelism Ministry Inc is a ministry that reaches out with the Gospel to children before and after birth. The ministry teaches and equips parents, teachers and coordinators of Sunday Schools and Children's Clubs. They also have and hold Children's Clubs, conferences and training seminars.

Focus on the Family
Tel: 1-800 - 232 6459
Website: www.family.org
Focus on the Family cooperates with the Holy Spirit in disseminating the Gospel of Jesus Christ to as many people as possible, and, specifically, to accomplish that objective by helping to preserve traditional values and the institution of the family.

Open Gate
2 Union Road
Croydon
CRO 2XU.
Tel: 0208 665 5533
Fax: 0208 684 7233
e-mail: opengate@yahoo.co.uk
　　　　alteschool@yahoo.co.uk
Open Gate Provides a preventative and supplementary educational facility for youths at risk of permanent exclusion. We aim at empowering and connecting the youths for the future. We provide support for the family and the community.

Protokos Publishers
P.O. Box 48424
London
SE15 2YL
www.protokospublishers.com
Protokos Publishers provides various resources for the family. We publish many life's enlightening, informative and motivational must read books. With each of our books, you are guaranteed a 24/7 counsellor by your side on the subject.

The Shepherd's Ministries
5 Brookehowse Road
Bellingham
London SE6 3TJ, UK
Tel/Fax: +44 208 698 7222
Email: info@theshepherdsministries.org
Website: www.theshepherdsministries.org
The Shepherd's Ministries helps to bring children into an experience of worshipping God in truth and in spirit; give children a world-view based on God's word and mission and helps children to exercise their gifts in local and global missions.

Useful Addresses

Teenagers' Outreach Ministries (TOM) Inc.
Plot 85
Ladi Kwali Ext. Layout,
P.O.Box 16
Kwali, Abuja.
Nigeria.
Tel- 02082933730
Fax-02082933731
Nigeria - 08037044195
         - 07081860407
Email- tominthq@yahoo.co.uk
Website -www.tominternational .org
The Teenagers' Outreach Ministries (TOM) Inc. has a vision of leading today's teenager to Christ. This forms the foundation on which we mould their character in line with the word of God, thereby equipping them to fulfil their God ordained roles in life.

Total Woman Ministries
The Total Woman Ministries,
3 Herringham Road
Thames Wharf Barrier,
Charlton,
London
SE7 8NJ.
Tel: 020 8293 3730
Fax: 020 8293 3731
Email: admin@totalwomanministries.org
Website:www.totalwomanministries.org
Total Woman Ministries by God's grace has the sole vision of reaching out to women of all categories (married, single, separated, divorced, young, middle-aged or elderly).

United Christian Broadcasting UCB
P.O. Box 255, Stoke on Trent,
ST4 8YY, England
Among other forms of spreading the Gospel, UCB prints The Word For Today – a free daily devotional reading available for residents in the UK and Republic of Ireland

Dear Reader,

Thank you for your time and resources committed to supporting this writing ministry. Please help to tell others about how much the Lord has blessed you reading this book.

You will certainly be blessed by the other books written by Oluwakemi, so why not visit www.protokospublishers.com and place an order today.

It will equally be appreciated if you can help to write a few sentences review of the book on www.amazon.com and / or on www.protokospublishers.com.

Please note that all our books are easily available on our website and other good bookshops.

God bless you as you do.
Management
Protokos Publishers.

www.ingramcontent.com/pod-product-compliance
Ingram Content Group UK Ltd.
Pitfield, Milton Keynes, MK11 3LW, UK
UKHW022209230426
12048UKWH00016BA/740